"Gave me goosebumps, made me teary. V

~ **Sue Bingham,** High Performance Work Group

"The future indeed will be awesome, but also uneven.
In fact, it's going to be downright unequal. In this provocative book,
Bill Jensen urges justness in our leadership.
His call to action is your duty to answer."
~ **Dan Pontefract,** best-selling author of *Open to Think*

"Bill Jensen is spot-on. Not enough leaders are thinking deeply
about the future of work and how it will affect those who do
that work. This fun but serious book will persuade more to do so.
We don't yet know how many jobs machines will take, but there's
no doubt that work is going to change a lot, and that people will
need a lot of help with the transformation."
~ **Thomas H. Davenport,** Research Fellow, MIT Initiative on the
Digital Economy, and author of *Only Humans Need Apply*

"Bill Jensen strips away the complex theories that so many of us
have grown up with and unveils powerful new perspectives and
opportunities that lie ahead for all.
An excellent read for students and teachers alike."
~ **Angela Maiers,** Founder, Choose2Matter

"*The Day Tomorrow Said No* is a refreshingly disruptive
take in the crowded dialogue about the future of work. Bill cuts
through the noise and offers a compelling and clean message
about not leaving people behind in a hyperdigitized world.
He offers hope for a more human future that speaks to us all!"
~ **Cecille Alper-Leroux,** Vice President,
Human Capital Innovation at Ultimate Software

"This wonderful book is about personal innovation applied to how we work. You can use these insights for the rest of your life. In all my experience in leading transformations, the biggest challenge has been in creating the future while doing today's work. *The Day Tomorrow Said No* addresses this challenge within a very compelling story."

~ **David Marlow,** former Director of Transformation and Innovation, Northwestern Mutual

"*The Day Tomorrow Said No* is an important book because it creates much-needed reflection space for conversations among leaders about the future of work. And those conversations, in turn, create diverse and inclusive future-focused mentoring for your teammates. Bill Jensen has written a fantastic story that helps every individual consider the path they are on and their role in the future."

~ **Joel Wright,** former Director, Learning and Innovation Solutions, Center for Creative Leadership

"*The Day Tomorrow Said No* reasonates with me on a very personal level. Each character is in a very different place. As leaders, that's where each of us needs to begin — by understanding what each individual is grappling with . . . what their fears and hopes are for the future. Bill Jensen has taken a highly complex issue — the future of work — and made it super-simple. This book's genius is in its simplicity!"

~ **Trudy Wonder,** Marketing Director, Ultimate Software

Published by Authors Place Press
9885 Wyecliff Drive, Suite 200
Highlands Ranch, CO 80126
Authorsplace.com

ISBN: 978-1-62865-711-1

THE DISCOVERY
THAT FOREVER CHANGED THE FUTURE
AND HOW WE WORK

The Day Tomorrow Said No

Bill Jensen

AUTHORS PLACE
— PRESS —

You Will Change the Future

Throughout human history,
every wicked challenge we've overcome
begins with a story.

Stories are how we make sense of things,
change hearts and minds,
clarify the complex,
and how we motivate people to take action.

THE DAY TOMORROW SAID NO
is one such story.

Each character is each of us.

Their journey is ours:
our transition into a new and amazing future.

Once you see yourself inside this story,
here is how it ends . . .

"I am accountable for _____."

This is your legacy moment.

The 21st century will be shaped by how you finish this story.
How you, and all of us, made fundamental shifts
in our mindsets and beliefs.

The World recently conspired to make
this book's fable very real.
Leaders: "There's no way we can shut everything down
and fix the future of work and other major societal problems."
World: "Here's a global virus . . .
Practice."

Now we must ask ourselves:
What is our social contract with each other?
Is it finally time to change things so no one gets left behind?
Do justice and purpose matter for all, or just for some?

The eyes of the future are looking back
to see what each of us did.

You will change the future.
Now, let's see how that begins.

Today, Tomorrow, and **Little One** —
the three magical forces of work —
keep the human race
moving forward.

Turning possibility
into capability
into legacy.

Today keeps us planning, doing, achieving.

He's the Get-It-Done force inside us all.

Tic, tic, tic.

Check, check, check.

Then passes our achievements on to Tomorrow.

Tomorrow gives us reasons to care.

Fiercely defending the space between

What Was and What Will Be,

she ignites our next day's To Dos

with passions, dreams, and imagination.

Little One prepares and mentors Team Future.

She's the force inside every next generation,

crazy creative, and radical rebel —

pushing us ever forward.

This is how it's always been.

Until . . .

Tomorrow said no.

She refused to take the daily hand-off.

Tomorrow said to Today . . .

> "You had one job.
> You didn't do it.
>
> You've set up eight billion people to fail.
> You're not handing off this mess to me!"

Tomorrow is running out of dreams.

Only one in ten
of Today's employees
can achieve their dreams
in their current jobs. [1]

Nine of every ten
workaday people . . .

The ones who do their jobs
with little fame or fanfare . . .

. . . watch as their dreams fade away.

Back burnered by MoreBetterFaster,
MoreBetterFaster.

She could not let that continue.

"Not on my watch!"
Tomorrow cried out.

Today harrumphed:

"We have plenty of dreamers,
dreaming big dreams!

Dreamers who are . . .
Taking us to Mars.
Caring for the needy.
Creating cars that think.
Reinventing education.
Extending life.

Dreamers who live life out loud!
With so much joy!

Tell her, Little One:
The future is limitless.
Anyone can do anything.
Everyone can be amazing."

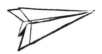

Little One replied . . .

"Yes, many will live in a future
beyond their wildest dreams!
And many will not.

Your fantastic future . . .
It's so unfairly, unevenly
distributed.

Too many dreams get stuck.
Too many people
left behind.

Today,
the great things
you're doing
aren't different enough,
soon enough,
for enough people."

The horrific global
pandemic of 2020
proved that.

"And if we don't act now,"
Little One continued,

"so many people's struggles
will get a lot worse.

In the next 20 years,
how people work
will change more
than in all of the past 2,000 years.[2]

That's a lifetime of change
every ten months!

How many on Team Future
can keep up with that?

How many of us will want to try?

Today, you must rethink
how check, check, checks
get done!"

Tomorrow jumped in . . .

"At the same time,
up to half of all jobs will
vanish.[3] Gone. Forever.

Replaced by what some call
the Robopocalypse:
Superintelligent automation
that radically changes
tasks and lives,
and why and how much
we pay people to work.

Two thirds of the youngest
Team Future teammates —
the ones in elementary school —
will work in jobs
that don't yet exist.[4]
And most everyone
who talks about this shift
gets it wrong."

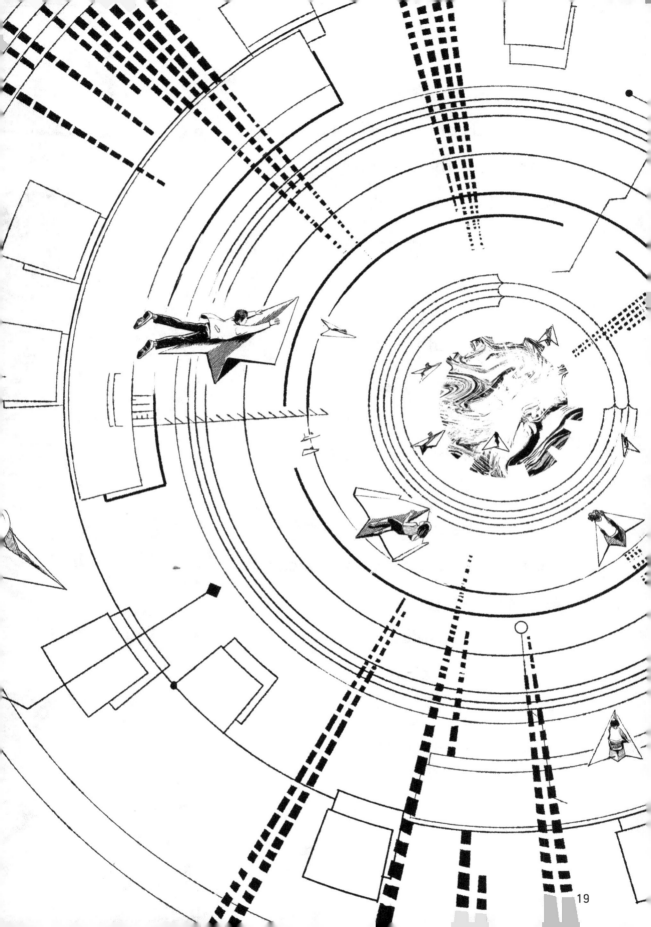

"'Don't worry,' they say.
New kinds of jobs will be created.
Better jobs than before!
All will be wonderful.

Except for . . .

The amount of trauma,
fear, and uncertainty
thrust upon
at least half of Team Future.

Because the rules for
income, opportunity, and success
are now changing hourly,
personal hardships will
erupt into social ills.

That puts everyone's future
at risk."

"Got it,"

Today asserted.

(He didn't really. Not yet.

Staying in his comfort zone meant sidestepping

the struggles of so many.)

He continued by — surprise! — assigning assignments . . .

"Tomorrow, you need more dreams.

Little One, you and Team Future

need new ways of working.

But the world also needs

to keep spinning.

My job is to make that happen.

So would you two

be our dream scouts?

Talk to those billions of people.

Find out what they need

to get us back on track."

Tomorrow and Little One cried out in unison:

"Will do!"

Tomorrow and Little One traveled the globe,
in deep conversations with everyone who works.

They asked robotmakers, bookkeepers,
and zookeepers about their passions.

They broke bread with bioengineers, gadgeteers,
and marketeers, asking: What truly matters?

Chatted with caterers and off-the-books laborers
about what makes them happy.

Debated global trends with data wranglers,
truck drivers, and warehouse managers.

Enjoyed the creations of entrepreneurs,
garment workers, and video game designers.

They learned about courage from women
gathering firewood to make cooking coal;
about empathy from healthcare workers;
about life from laboratory assistants
and mid-managers in mega companies.

They were deeply moved and impressed
by what they found.

More love than fear.
More pulling together than pushing apart.

More determination than resignation.
More joyful anticipation than despair.

So much hope for a wonderful future!
For everyone, and for their children's children.

They were also deeply saddened and concerned by what they found.

Unsustainable volatility, uncertainty, confusion, and disillusionment.

Three in four see the future of work pushing them to their outer limits, beyond their capacity.[5]

Arrrrrgh!

Tomorrow and Little One
toiled to make sense of
the conflicting complexities.

Purpose, passion, values,
family, community, and creativity
are the most powerful driving forces.
Those beliefs and ideals
build intensely beautiful dreams.

Yet for so many,
the demands of the daily grind
exceed their reach for dreams.
More breakdowns than breakthroughs.

They thought long and hard . . .

Scribbling ideas, tossing them aside,
starting over . . .

Until finally,
they were ready to share what they found
with Today.

They had hoped for happy anticipation.

Instead, Today was in full-on harrumph mode,
barely looking up from check-check-checking.

Little One and Tomorrow would not be deterred.
This was too important.

"We need to reboot how we think
about the design of work,"
Tomorrow began.

"Sure, there are billions of jobs,
and countless ways to earn a living . . .

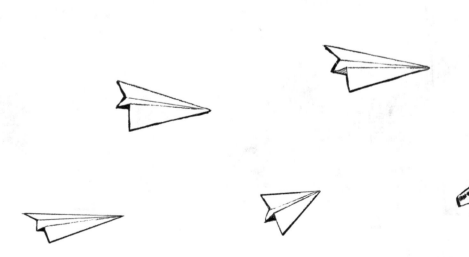

But buried within all job titles,

teams, and tasks,

are **only three kinds** of work;

three kinds of workers and leaders.

Rebooting with these three roles

will spark the biggest explosion

of human capacity, ever."

Little One jumped in . . .

"Believers. Breakers. Builders!
Everybody who works,
no matter their job, or title,
or experience,
is either a . . .

Believer,

        Breaker,

               or Builder.

These roles are universal.
Your skills, your duties,
and your tasks will change.
But the 3Bs guide you
through a crazy, disrupted world.
They keep you true to you.
The 3Bs are how to Be.

They are the real reasons
daily possibilities
get turned into capabilities,
and into lasting legacies."[6]

"Believers,"

Tomorrow continued,

"are passionate everyday people
who tirelessly toil to make their dreams
come true, and who protest
when current systems don't work.

Today, you may not want them
up in your face . . ."
(He most definitely did not) . . .

"But dreams only come true if Believers
believe they can.
Believers are the force
that keeps hope alive.
Their passions fan the embers
of other people's fading dreams.

Even when their days are difficult,
they still cry out: 'I have a dream.' [7]

And Believers cheer the loudest
when things do change!"

"Breakers are passionate pioneers
who break with the past
and reimagine what's possible.

Here's to the crazy ones,
the misfits and rebels,
the travelers into the future,
rule-breaking,
truth-facing
trailblazers.[8]

They break us away
from our limiting beliefs,
create new paths for
life to expand.
They create new objects,
experiences,
and journeys for us all.

But not fully.
We still need one more group
to finish the bridge to the future."

"**Builders** are fiery leaders
who reimagine entire systems.

Big systems like
clean energy, water,
and tackling poverty, disease,
and societal conflict.

Little systems like
how teams and organizations
come together.
Systems that no one owns,
and everyone owns.

Builders are makers and disruptors
who create new ways of being.
They make the impossible, possible.

And Builders have the vision
and the responsibility
to create roles for
Breakers and Believers
in those new ways of being."

Tomorrow concluded,

"To keep the human race moving forward,
everyone has a 3B responsibility.

No matter the job,
everyone's tasks must be driven
by at least
one of these roles.

You can even be all three!

From now on,
everyone not only
has the duties of their job,
but also
Believer, Breaker, or Builder
responsibilities.

Everyone is responsible
for everyone's future."

"I have a . . ."
Today began, but Little One jumped in:

"Do you not get
that everyone's future
depends on this?!
Your way doesn't work!"

"As I started to say,"
Today continued . . .
"I have a question."

"Oh,"
Little One muttered.

"Tomorrow and Little One,
this is incredible!"

Their smiles grew so big that their cheeks ached!

"But . . . How?
How do we reboot everything
while I still keep everyone
check, check, checking?"

Tomorrow continued,

"All things digital and all measures
are built to revolve around
at least one of these 3B passions.

All leaders and companies
and products and services
invoke, push for, and support
one or more of the 3Bs.

All education, training,
development
must help people understand
and perform with 3B skills.

All that will take time.

Right now, it's up to us three
to grow our tribes."

"Little One needs to educate,

motivate, and support

Team Future teammates

in taking on

their 3B responsibilities.

"I need to grow the dreams

we have stockpiled

to create a pull so powerful

that lots more dreamers

join our 3B movement.

And you, dear Today,
need to create the space for
all your Check-Check-Checkers
to talk about their dreams.
Help people with conversations
about their hopes and fears,
dreams and passions.

If we do that,
the 3Bs will begin to take off."

"And when this works,"
Tomorrow wrapped up,

"Today, you'll be the hero!

We'll be remembered as dream scouts.

You'll be remembered

as the one who made work work."

"I'm in!"
Today declared.

High-fives all around!

Then Today asked . . .

"But . . . The billions of souls
who were struggling . . .
What's their responsibility?
How do they help themselves?"

Tomorrow replied:

"It's up to us, all of us,
to create better tomorrows.

Everyone who has dreams,
who wants to dream bigger dreams . . .
who wants more happiness, autonomy,
fulfillment . . .

Everyone who's concerned about the future,
or wants a more amazing future . . .

Everyone who has little ones of their own,

Or who is someone's little one . . .

Everyone who's busy check-check-checking . . .

Everyone who hears or reads this message . . .

Now must choose . . ."

Which of the 3Bs will you be?

Believer, Breaker, or Builder?

When will you start?
What will you do?

We Can Solve This

The Day Tomorrow Said Yes!

Tomorrow's story is our story. She changed the conversation, and took back the future. We can and must do the same.

"I am accountable for _____ ."

We'll take back our future as we fill in that blank.
That begins by changing the conversation.

Back Story

CALL TO ACTION

Be accountable for changing the conversation
that changes the future.
For you. And for those we're leaving behind.
Create conversations that address, not ignore,
our most wicked challenges.

We are now faced with the fact that tomorrow is today.
We are confronted with the fierce urgency of now.
~ Martin Luther King Jr.

Why I Wrote This Book

You have lived through a global dumpster-fire.

A perfect storm of destructive and disruptive forces that few could have ever imagined.

And definitive proof that our education, business, and economic systems were designed to leave far too many people behind.

As well as . . .
No better proof that our human spirit is indefatigable, indestructible, and infinitely resilient. The sublime beauty of our humanity has emerged from the chaos. Communities, ingenuity, and love sprouted everywhere.

All that and lots more flowed from the pandemic of 2020. Suddenly, across the globe, everything changed. Including our shared future.

The 2020 corona-virus displaced more than 90% of the world's children from their schools.[9] More than one-third of the planet's population was under some form of lockdown.[10] The monthly unemployment total for mid-March to mid-April was 22 million U.S. jobs lost — wiping out a decade-worth of job gains,[11] and by midyear the U.S. economy posted its worst drop — ever.[12]

An Oxfam report said that by the time the pandemic is over, its impact could thrust half of the world's population into poverty.[13] In the U.S., more than half of the working poor, especially Black and Latino households, reported serious financial problems due to the effects of coronavirus,[14] losing their jobs at a rate eight times greater than higher-wager earners.[15]

"This is what an epidemic shows us," said German Chancellor Angela Merkel. "How vulnerable we all are, how dependent on the considerate behaviors of others. These are not simply abstract numbers or statistics. [The virus's victims are] someone's father or grandfather, a mother or grandmother, a partner. They are people. And we are a community in which every life and every person matters."[16]

That's why I wrote this book: To tell a simple yet powerful story of how interconnected we all are, how we all succeed or fail together, and, as we must now leap into a post-coronavirus future, that we're still leaving far too many people behind.

Welcome to Our Never-Normal-Again Future
While the virus is a devastatingly lethal weapon, it did not cause these global ravages and challenges. We did. In how we built our economy, our companies, our work, our systems, and our priorities. "Let's not minimize the negatives. This is very tough on a lot of people," said CNN anchor Fareed Zakaria, when asked to emphasize the positive opportunities created by this crisis. "Unfortunately, the part that we're going to find more difficult than people are imagining is finding that Restart Button."[17]

#We'reAllInThisTogether declared every politician, CEO, and celebrity feel-good video. But are we really? Are we willing to make the necessary changes? As the New York Times asked:

We can't return to normal, because the normal that we had was precisely the problem.

COVID-19 graffiti in Hong Kong

"What kind of economy will emerge from the crisis? Will it be one that continues to create inequalities . . . Or will it be one that honors the dignity of work, rewards contributions to the real economy, gives workers a meaningful voice and shares the risks of ill health and hard times?"[18]

Canadian Prime Minister Justin Trudeau warned that our systems have been failing us for a long time: "The world is in a crisis. . . Not just because of COVID-19. But because of the last few decades. . . . Things are about to get much worse unless we change."[19]

We cannot return to normal. Because normal was always designed to leave far too many people behind. If our goal is to go back to how things were, we will have lost the valuable lessons we were just taught. We must be thoughtful about what we bring back, and courageous about what we create anew.

The Future That Was
We are dancing on the edge of one of the most magnificent and transformative moments in history. All things digital once held the promise of a future that would be better than anyone could imagine: 3D printed houses and bridges, deep analytics curing diseases in record time, a surgeon replacing an organ when she's half a planet away, third-world farmers using their phones to triple crop yield, roads and walkways that generate power . . . Wow! The possibilities for that future are (still) truly limitless!

And . . . It is utterly unacceptable that so many of us are being left behind. We need to reimagine digital transformation to be far better economic and societal transformations for us all.

The eyes of the future are looking back at us, demanding that we get this moment right.

When work becomes the killer of dreams it's time to redream our work.

Among Today, Tomorrow, and Little One: Tomorrow's crisis is very real. The idea for this book began over four years ago. During my future-of-work research, I asked people a question no one else was asking: "Can you achieve your dreams where you currently work?" Less than ten percent of those in the middle and frontlines of organizations said yes.[20] That is unacceptable.

When work becomes the killer of dreams, it's time to redream our work.

I wrote this book as a call to action:
To change the conversation about, and the leadership of,
the future of work.

In most organizations, the future of work has become an overused banality — a self-driving, robotized meme. Too many leaders are deliberately ignoring the most difficult and crucial conversations.

Business leaders have not reimagined the people dimensions of work fast enough, aggressively enough. The amount of disruption in innovation, automation, globalization, and efficiency far exceeds the much-needed disruptions in how we lead, structure, and develop people.

Some examples: While your surgery can now be performed with robotics, medical resident training on those tools is so bad that it's life-threatening.[21] While augmented reality (AR) is revolutionizing education,[22] many of our teachers are forced to work up to six jobs just to get by.[23] While tech is our future, right now a Facebook employee in San Francisco is sleeping in her car because she cannot afford a place to live in the Bay Area.[24] While disruptors are creating driverless cars and trucks, New York City taxi driver suicides recently hit one per month, because they saw no way to support their families, no path forward.[25]

The World Economic Forum says that a reskilling revolution is

The biggest barrier
to an amazing future
for all:
Past-due
mindset shifts

absolutely required to keep up with future needs,[26] and industry-watchers tell us that this revolution is happening far too slowly.[27] [28] "Every company is doing something in this area," said J.P.Morgan CEO Jamie Dimon, "but it's got to be ten times more."[29]

This was made abundantly clear to millions of workers who suddenly realized how much of their work could be done from home! Century-old norms of we-must-be-in-the-office were decimated within months — instantly creating completely new workplace expectations.[30]

The urgency of this book grew out of the disturbing emergence of a bipolar economy. One of the world's 100 richest people, Ray Dalio, warns that we're creating an economy where the middle class is eradicated, and we will soon be divided into the top 40% and the bottom 60%.[31] Within that top 40%, the richest 1% will own two-thirds of all wealth by 2030.[32] Early signs of this 40/60 split are already here: A full-time minimum wage earner in the US cannot afford to rent a two-bedroom apartment *anywhere* in the entire country.[33] Also, the first weeks of the coronavirus showed how much hardship there is for so many in missing just one paycheck.

And from this recent *New York Times* article, "Tech is Splitting the U.S. Workforce in Two": "There is a small island of highly educated professionals making good wages at corporations like Intel or Boeing, which reap hundreds of thousands of dollars in profit per employee. That island sits in the middle of a sea of less educated workers who are stuck at businesses like hotels, restaurants, and nursing homes that generate much smaller profits per employee and stay viable primarily by keeping wages low."[34]

Yet the foundational problem is not economics.

**"We already talked about this.
We're on top of this."**

- -

**Understand how little
we still understand.**

Win the race to wisdom.

**Ask the questions
no one else is asking.**

It's in how capitalism is practiced — our lack of care and accountability for all who are left behind.[35]

Says economist Paul Collier, "Modern capitalism has the potential to lift us all to unprecedented prosperity, but it is morally bankrupt and on track for tragedy. If capiltalism is to work for everyone, it needs to be managed so as to deliver purpose as well as productivity."[36]

From the video *Humans Need Not Apply*, which details the coming AI/robot revolution: "History shows us: Workers always lose, economics always wins. We need to start thinking now about what to do when large sections of the population are unemployable through no fault of their own. What to do in a future where, for most jobs, humans need not apply."[37]

If we do not change our trajectory, historian Yuval Noah Harari warns that an AI era could create a "global useless class."[38] We cannot allow that to happen.

I wrote this book to expose the future of work's hidden underbelly. One of the biggest challenges we face is that the Fourth Industrial Revolution[39] — driven by AI, robots, and augmentation — has no face. Or country. No one to be held accountable, or to take responsibility for harmful consequences.

Which means those who are struggling to create and control their own destiny will not rise up against our robots and algorithms. They will take their fear, anger, and vulnerability out on immigrants and foreigners, nations and nonbelievers, police and teachers, flight attendants and cashiers.

This has already begun. Rage and fears about societal shifts, automation, and globalization are being directed at whoever isn't part of the same tribe, look like us, or who just doesn't seem to

"Our future is limitless, abundant, amazing!"

(NOT WITHOUT)

Caring about how many we're leaving behind.

Caring about how many 'off our books' costs are offloaded onto so many others.

care. If we do not act quickly, deep societal divides will be intensified and last for decades.[40] [41] [42] [43]

"People are trying desperately, mightily to cope. By whatever means they can," says Umair Haque, author of *Betterness: Economics for Humans.* "A kind of trauma-bomb . . . has gone off across society. Traumatized every day by an age that will punch, slap, kick, and trample them, before it will hold, touch, or lift them.[44] We need transformational empathy, concern, dignity. "[45]

Is this traumapocalypse, as economist Haque calls it, happening everywhere, to everyone? Of course not. The future is going to be amazing . . . right? Of course it is. For some. But not all.

Far too many of us — up to half — are being left behind. Far too many of us feel mostly confusing trauma coming at us from the disruptive future. Occasionally, there are life-altering traumas — like most of us experienced during the coronavirus crisis. But usually, there's just a daily, constant drumbeat of mini-traumas destroying focus, hope, and possibilities.

Education, we are told, is key. Those who can learn how to be lifetime learners will not be so traumatized.

Founder of Singularity University, Ray Kurzweil, says that this is the leap we must make in education and corporate training and development: "Curriculum will focus on critical survival skills, such as leading by influence, agility and adaptability, initiative and entrepreneurship, effective communication, analyzing information, and curiosity and imagination. [Education, training and development must be] focused on robot-proofing our youth [and workforce], and helping them leverage technology in ways that can help solve the grand challenges facing our species."[46]

How we currently develop and train people is lightyears from

Kurzweil's model. (Just ask any teacher, trainer, or coach about their daily challenges with 2020 Zoom chats and Google Classrooms!) Yet that disruptive future is already here: By 2025, machines will do more work than humans![47] We *must* radically alter the conversation we're having, and how we're approaching this dilemma!

So many costs of this new future — how to robotproof and disrupt oneself at warp speed, societal conflict, economic class polarization, personal vulnerability and risks — are thrust upon each individual and ignored by most organizations. These "off our books" costs are not discussed in boardrooms. The costs for amazing futures for the few are being offloaded onto the many. And that offloading will only increase. Unless there's pushback.

Before we pushback on or transform anything — we first must bear witness to, and feel the pain and struggles of, all those we're leaving behind. If we do, we'll soon begin to understand that there is no *them*, only *all of us*.

I wrote this book for all, not just for some. I wrote this book in this format — easily read and used by anyone at any age — because a lot of that pushback will come from today's youth, the true Team Future. The work and learning systems we're building now are impacting their future.

"Young people . . . are looking at the world around them and calling BS. They are leading movements and demanding accountability," says Julia LaSalvia, a self-proclaimed member of the selfie generation.[48] "Should we teach our children to be activists?" asks Caroline Paul, author of *The Gutsy Girl*. "Yes, definitely. Now."[49]

While *Tomorrow Said No* is a leadership and business book, we also tested it with middle schoolers and up. One thirteen year-old girl with autism spectrum disorder excitedly shared, "I loved this book so much! I related to it so much! I saw me and my future in it."[50]

> *We'll rise up*
> *In spite of the ache*
> *We'll rise up*
> *And we'll do it a thousand times again*
> *~ "Rise Up," Andra Day*

Most importantly:
I wrote this book to create a new path to hope, redemption, and more amazing futures for us all.

I truly believe that the future can and will be AMAZING! But not the way all that needs to be done is being sidestepped. We *must* pay attention to those offloaded heartaches, struggles, and massive off-our-books costs and consequences.

To address them, we must all own our 3B roles.

Believers, Breakers, and Builders are very real roles for our path forward. We, individually and in our communities, must take on greater responsibilities so that the future of work works for all, not just some.

The **Believer** role is crucial. No one gets to passively experience work, the future, or their place in it. Each of us must actively design our place in that future, and what guides our experience. Hope. Optimism. Passion. Purpose. Courage. Self-efficacy. Taking action. Taking care of each other. Each of these is an essential personal responsibility. Each of us has a role in energizing ourselves, as well as others.

Like the recent #MeToo, #MyLifeMatters, #SecureOurFuture,

**The future is being created
by leaders, techies, disruptors,
innovators, robots, and AI.**

(NOT WITHOUT ALL OF US)

**The workforce
and lifelong learners
must co-design
the future as
Believers, Breakers, Builders.**

#MarchforOurLives and #FamiliesBelongTogether movements, what's needed is lots more grassroots activism to get business to change faster. Bottom-up activists taking stands for how people are treated, cared for, led, structured, supported, trained, and developed in an AI-driven world. We need to do more to ensure that all of us have a say in where this new world is taking us. Market forces alone within the war for talent still leave far too many behind.

We need lots more activism and advocacy for those who are truly struggling due to business's approach to the future of work. A lot of that activism will come from Little One's tribe, Team Future — the next generation who have to live the longest with Today's problem-filled handoff.

We have a real-life model for Little One: Teenage Swedish student activist and Believer Greta Thunberg. "Our house is on fire," she passionately shared, dismissing the usual admonishments that addressing climate change is very complex, that reforms are hard, and that solutions take time. "Either we avoid chain reaction of unraveling ecosystems, or we don't. . . . We all have a choice: We can either create transformational action or continue with business as usual and fail. . . . I don't want your hope. I want you to act."[51]

Just like Greta Thunberg does for our planet, we need passionate activists to push back on how many people are being left behind by how companies strive for *morebetterfaster*. Activists who will not accept ". . . but the solutions are complex and hard." Who keep reminding us that our how-we-work house is on fire. Activists who push us to act faster and more fully.

Workforce activism absolutely works in getting companies to change. And workers are using a company's own data to force those changes.

**The fierce urgency of tomorrow
starts today.**

**Everyone is responsible
for everyone's future.**

**Ability to
achieve one's dreams,
create and control
one's own future,
are central to
the future of all work.**

Every current and potential employee can go to Glassdoor.com to discover a company's best/worst reviews. They can also go to PipelineEquity.com to see how companies are addressing gender biases in hiring and career growth. Or they can find a company's cultural ranking through Glassdoor/Sloan Management Review's Culture 500 tool — tracking company cultures across nine separate sets of values. Or they can use Deloitte research that says the average Net Promoter score for Training and Development is -8% (horrible), and ask for their prospective employer's score.

We also need future of work activism from our organizational leaders. "The power of being in the leadership position [is] that you can influence an ecosystem," said HP CEO Dion Weisler. "You can step up and lead across [an entire business ecosystem] to make a difference in the things you really believe in."[52] To signal support for such a move, CEOs within The Business Roundtable — America's largest companies — recently signed up to end share-holder primacy and to invest more deeply in their employees.[53] [54]

Whatever your role, I've compiled workshops, how to guides, and video tutorials on what you can do immediately to change your future and our shared future. Like . . .
- Becoming a passionate activist
- Learning four core future-of-work skillsets
- Changing what we track and measure
- Changing how we approach learning and performance
- Changing how we approach agency, empowerment

For free and cheap leadership, training, and personal performance toolkits, go to www.TomorrowSaidY.es.

"The fierce urgency of now" is upon us. When Dr. King spoke those words, he also asked, "[W]ill there be [a] message . . . of hope, of solidarity with their yearnings, of commitment to their cause, whatever the cost? The choice is ours . . ."[55]

The man who marched with Dr. King, Congressman John Lewis, epitomized a true Believer's passion: "When you see something that is not right, not fair, not just, say something! Do something! Get in trouble. Good trouble. Necessary trouble."[56]

We must begin solving for short-term *and* long-term needs. We cannot keep ignoring how so many of today's disruptions create tomorrow's problems.

I grew up in New York State, where the five Iroquois nations shaped the ideas that would later become foundational to United States democracy. We clearly have ignored the intent behind the Great Law of the Iroquois Confederacy: "In our every deliberation, we must consider the impact of our decisions on the next seven generations."[57]

The choice is ours. We cannot blow this opportunity!

The great news: We already have some passionate **Breakers** and **Builders** we can learn from, who are already reimagining how we work.

Look at *Fortune*'s or Glassdoor's "Best Place to Work" lists and you'll find many new best practices. As well as amazing new ideas in learning and development from the Breakers and Builders at Singularity University; IDEO; Khan Academy; New Jersey's St. Benedict's Prep, where students have run the school as part of their education and development since the 1970s[58]; and Finland, which became the first country to eliminate all subjects, and instead study events — such as understanding math, geography, art, music, and history through the lens of events in the students lives.

The still-urgent crisis: **We just don't have enough of these 2Bs to go around**. We need to find, nurture, and grow lots more

Breakers and Builders. Everywhere. In every company, every school, and in every of area of coaching and development.

We need far more disruptive heroes breaking and rebuilding worksystems. Fast. Now.

"Policy makers . . . and companies . . . will need to show bold leadership . . . in the mammoth task of reskilling people (for AI)," says McKinsey. "Individuals will need to adjust to . . . the needs in a dynamically changing job market.[59] Between 400 million and 800 million individuals could be displaced by automation and need to find new jobs by 2030."[60]

Recognizing this, Amazon recently pledged to upskill 100,000 US employees for in-demand jobs by 2025.[61] That's great, but AI will have far-reaching impacts beyond the top five tech companies: Facebook, Apple, Amazon, Netflix, and Google.

After a recent Stanford University summit on the Future of AI, *Fortune* magazine declared "[AI] will transform society in ways we have only begun to imagine — both for good and for bad. Among the big questions that have to be grappled with:

- How do we deal with job market disruption as the nature of work is transformed? All the [summit's] participants . . . worried about the massive retraining needed to survive the transition.
- How do we address the inequality that stems from the winner-take-most nature of the digital technology revolution?"[62]

This is a solvable crisis! We can learn how to do all this from Today, Tomorrow, and Little One. And from what they learned about Believers, Breakers, and Builders.

Tomorrow's story is our story. She stood up to Today, pushing back. Accompanied by Little One — who represents our future generations — she changed the conversation. Changed Today's focus and priorities to create a new path forward. Now, they pass that responsibility onto us.

The fierce urgency of tomorrow starts today.

The future of work is now.

Which of the 3Bs will you be?

What will you be accountable for?

Whether you act or do nothing, you are shaping your future and the future of others.

How will you speak up?

We must bend the arc of the future toward all dreams, not just dreams for some of us.

The greatest practical bravery of our times is daring to radically change the conversation about work so tomorrow is better for us all.

The Journey to Tomorrow's

Begins with Changing the Conversation

Facilitator's Guide

GOAL: To change the conversation about the future of work.
To make it easier for each person to assume
new accountabilities.
By leading conversations that address, not ignore,
our most wicked challenges.
Leading to new understandings, new choices, new actions.

ROLE: Facilitate an open, flowing, no-judgment conversation.
No right or wrong answers.
Exploring new ideas and views about the future.
Creating meaning-making, deeper understanding.

QUESTIONS:
SELECT THREE OR FOUR OF THE FOLLOWING

OVERALL

• After reading *The Day Tomorrow Said No:*
What is your biggest takeaway about the future of work?
What was your biggest "Aha"?

WHAT'S YOUR VIEW? SHOULD IT CHANGE?

• This book describes rapid, unprecedented personal disruptions.
— similar to the coronavirus crisis. Some people will be left
behind, are fearful, or are really struggling.
Others will feel that the disruptions are no big deal
or are very positive.
What's your view?
How will these disruptions impact you, personally? How soon?
How will they impact others who matter to you?

(Faciliation note: All views are valid.
Help people truly hear and empathize with differing points of view.
Help people see how anxiety or inequality or lack of opportunity or development
impacts many others, not just one individual.)

WHO IS MOST LIKE THE CURRENT YOU?

• Which character — Today, Tomorrow, or Little One —
did you most identify with? And why?

THE BIGGEST UNDISCUSSABLE

• Tomorrow and Little One tried to get Today to pay attention
to issues he just didn't want to discuss.
After reading this book:
What's the biggest undiscussable in your organization or team
that absolutely must be addressed to prepare you and your teammates
for a wildly disruptive future?

WHICH 3B ARE YOU?

• Tomorrow and Little One discover the secret — that we all
have a role as either Believers, Breakers, or Builders.
Which of the 3Bs best describes you? And why?

IS GREATER ACTIVISM NEEDED?

• Being a Believer was defined as having an activist's role.
In the author's prologue, he made the case for activism.
Do you believe activism about the future of work is necessary?
If yes, how? In what areas?
What is your activist's role and responsibility?

WHAT'S YOUR BIG DREAM?

• In your 3B role, what idea for the future inspires you,
excites you?
What's your "moon shot" — your big dream for an
amazing future — that you'd like to make happen?

WHAT NOW?

• At the end of the book the author says:
The fierce urgency of tomorrow starts now.
What could you [. . . or we . . .] work on immediately that would
be the first steps toward the dream futures
you just discussed?

CLOSE: When appropriate, discuss next steps — who does what.
Refer everyone to the online Getting Started toolkits and
source for upcoming best practice communities:
www.TomorrowSaidY.es

Getting to

Yes!

How Your Conversations Change the Future

All futurists have a crucial role: to create new and different conversations so we can see new possibilities and make new decisions. I discussed the use of this book as a conversation tool with dozens of futurists. One of them is Sohail Inayatullah, UNESCO Chair in Future Studies at UNESCO and USIM.

"Most conversations reinforce our current views," shared Sohail. "Usually, leaders of organizations, cities, and countries want some kind of proof and certainty that would cause them to change. And they want specific advice on what to do. Instead of giving them that kind of advice or certainty, I frame conversations for a learning transformation journey. I help them challenge their assumptions, which are locking them into certain ways of thinking and acting. Often, I use storytelling and narratives — like *The Day Tomorrow Said No* — to help them come to new conclusions, and change their strategies and behaviors."

This approach is echoed by Priya Parker, founding member of the Sustained Dialogue Campus Network, member of the World

Economic Forum Values Council, and one of the 100 disruptive heroes I interviewed for my sixth book, *Disrupt!*

Priya's 2019 TED Talk on how to turn everyday get-togethers into transformative gatherings [63] has been viewed over two million times. In her talk, she lists three steps in creating a transformative conversation:

> **1. Embrace a specific disputable purpose.**
> For example, this book opened with a purpose, a reason to change: We're leaving too many people behind. Few would dispute that assertion. But the spectrum of possible solutions *is* debatable.

> **2. Cause good controversy.**
> Instead of taking sides with dueling opinions, tell stories. Explore the differences and similarities of what's behind each of those stories. Which is exactly why *The Day Tomorrow Said No* was written this way. And exactly what Tomorrow and Little One did as dream scouts.

> **3. Create temporary rules for alternative conversations.**
> Temporary norms that make it OK for us to change our assumptions. That's the role of your conversations after reading this book: Exploring new ways of thinking and being.

Here's why these kinds of conversations are crucial: Things are BOTH getting better — the future will be amazing! — AND many people will be hurt and left broken by how we create that future. Both views are correct. We need more conversations that acknowledge BOTH of these truths, *together*. And address BOTH truths, equally, with equal attention, resources, and urgency.

TED is renowned for creating that kind of conversation. So is the MIT Media Lab. Each year they offer the Disobedience Award [64] —

a $250,000 prize to the person or group who truly changed our conversation by changing the rules. Criteria for winning: nonviolence, creativity, and personal responsibility (I am accountable for _____.). It's about speaking truth to power and demanding systemic change. (Believer, Breaker.)

That's our role after reading this book.

Not disobedience in the traditionally bad sense. But in creating the safe and passionate space for today's undiscussables: that too many dreams are being left behind; that too many people are being left behind; that positive changes aren't happening quickly enough for enough people; that we each have new responsibilities for a more wonderful future for all.

Design firm IDEO uses this kind of conversation to jumpstart its designs — writing a new and different story about the future by answering the question, "What future do we want to create?"[65]

Throughout human history, every wicked challenge we've overcome begins with a story. *The Day Tomorrow Said No* is one such story.

Now, it's up to each of us to carry this story forward. Make it our own.

This is our legacy moment. Your legacy moment too.

The 21st century will be shaped by how you finish this story.

Databank

ACKNOWLEDGMENTS

These are the people who kept me grounded as I pursued my crazy dreams and passions with this book. **Thank you so much!**

Family and Friends. You made me laugh, kinda sane, and loved me, no matter what. I couldn't have done this without your love and support!

I dedicate this book to my sister, Laura, and her husband, Russ, and their kids, Marc, Jolene, Brittany, and Courtney, whose amazing love and pure tenacity are helping Laura conquer her health issues. We're gonna kick that brain aneurism's butt!

From Rough Idea to Final Product Teammates. As I've never before attempted a book like this, my learning curve was steep. So I reached out to old and new friends for help. From helping me shape the rough idea, to refining it, to Kickstarter supporters who believed in and helped fund part of this dream, to testing it in corporate and educational settings — huge thanks to the superheroes who made this dream a reality . . .

Mark Babbitt, Craig Bardeneuer, Chris Beer, Tami Belt, Alisha Bhagat, Brent Biedermann, Mark Binder, Wally Bock, Dennis Bonilla, Marge Brady, Rebecca Braitling, Janine Buis, Papitha Cader, Joe Caserta, Todd Cherches, Nitzan Cohen Arazi, Carol Cole-Lewis, Eric Crowter, Suzanne Daigle, Anika Embrechts, Chris Ernst, John Estafanous, the entire Everett family — Jessica, Micah, Rachel, Noah, Josiah, Leah, Emma Phyllis Frazer, Michelle French, Dave Gray.

As well as Adam Hansen, Teresa Haggerty, John Harvey, Lisa Hesmondhalgh, Diane Hewat, Liz Curtis Higgs, Jon Husband, Steph Janssen, Dawna Jones, Cathy Keaulani, Doug Kirkpatrick, Jaco Koster, Howard Kraft, Smadar Krampf, Mathieu Laferriere, Vaidy Lakshminarayanpuram, François Lavallée, Joy Lindsay, Rob Maas, Lindy Mantin, Jean Marrapodi, Carles Marti, Nevin Mays, Mina McBride, Eileen McDargh, William McKnight, Bernard Mohr, Kate North, Olga Livshin, Tara Orlowski, Carla Perrotta, David Physick, Shauna Pollock and her entire class at the Blue Sky School, Ed Rankin, Kent Reyling, Jeff Rogers.

As well as Rosemary Scholz, Suzanne Schraeder, Kathy Shalhoub, Carmen Simons, Marilyn Sims, Camille Smith, Doug Smith, Annie Snowbarger, Linda Stamato, Faith Teeple, Perry Timms, Steve Tout, Pat Turnbull, David Underwood, Julie Winkle Giulioni, Ross Wirth, Mike Wittenstein, Jason Womack, Trudy Wonder, Joel Wright, Andrea Zintz, Mary Zisk, Michal Ziso.

Thanks guys!

Book Teammates. Nothing in this book would have been possible without the amazing artwork by Yuko Fukushima and Mihato, as well as the wonderful support of Authors Place, headed by Tony Ferraro and Steve Lavey. Amazing AP teammates include Joseph Emnace, London Koffler, Erahn Martin, Jonathan Prisant, Teri Whitten. Huge thanks to the entire team!

You. This book is nothing without your Ahas, your conversations, and actually putting it to use. Thank you for adding that missing ingredient!

FOOTNOTES, ENDNOTES

1. Jensen Group future of work research, 2014—ongoing. "Can you achieve your dreams where you currently work?" asked of over 20,000 people globally. (In Likert-scale surveys, as well as interviews and focus groups.) Overall results, less than one-third, 29% respondent favorably.

But that score was that "high" because it included senior execs, entrepreneurs, and those individuals most likely able to achieve their dreams no matter where they worked. For those who were mid-level and below, not working in startups, or tech firms, or smaller firms with entrepreneurial cultures, only 9.8% responded favorably.

Tomorrow's and Little One's dream scout journey mirrors what we found in follow-up interviews: People's desire to dream and achieve their dreams and personal goals has not diminished. But keeping up with overload, disruption, and churn, coupled with their inability to create and control their own destiny, those dreams and personal goals seemed out of reach for so many.

2. Maurice Conti, Chief Innovation Officer, Alpha, 20 > 2000: http://bit.ly/2pY1uOY

3. Oxford University, 47% of jobs disappearing due to automation: http://bit.ly/2GoYYvl. OECD study, nearly half of all jobs are vulnerable to automation: https://econ.st/2HBDYyi.

On the lower end of job loss estimates, McKinsey says it will be over a fifth of the global workforce, or 800 million people: https://mck.co/2KfoTnC. Whether you go high or low, that's still far too many people impacted without proper to support to bring them into the future of work.

And the most crucial conversation we should be having is not the debate over whether it will be this many or that many job losses. It's how pay scales and work opportunities overall will be affected. Even in the recent report by Barclays, http://bit.ly/2ra6PDs, which argues that some job opportunities will grow due to AI automation, they concede: "Middle skill workers are likely to be negatively affected, including through depressed wage prospects." Similarly, Brookings found, https://brook.gs/2Kqf1HS, that while automation may not produce as many net job losses as some fear, since the early 2000s, automation as reduced workers' share of national income.

The crucial conversation needs to be about how many people we are leaving behind, and that doing so will create many major societal and economic problems.

4. Primary schoolers and jobs, World Economic Forum: http://bit.ly/2H2vOzv

5. Three in four beyond their capacity: Ultimate Software/Jensen 2018 study on future of work, future of HR http://bit.ly/2NDhXkS

6. 3Bs inspired by a 2017 post by Umair Hague: Burners, Breakers, Believers, and Builders http://bit.ly/2FUV8XG. While his post went in a slightly different direction, we are absolutely are on the same page on this: "We need more, better rebellion. It isn't enough, what we're doing now."

7. Inspired by Martin Luther King Jr's "I Have a Dream" speech, "I say to you today, my friends, even though we face the difficulties of today and tomorrow, I still have a dream." http://bit.ly/2Gqsv3P

8. Inspired by Apple ad: http://bit.ly/2H0VQTD

9. 90% of children displaced by coronavirus: https://bit.ly/2RrpEzn

10. Coronavirus, more than one-third of planet on lockdown: https://bit.ly/3b2glZ6

11. 22 million file for U.S. unemployment in one month: https://wapo.st/2wSyWNK

12. U.S. economy posts its lowest drop ever: https://cnn.it/34iO8k0

13. Oxfam report on global poverty due to COVID-19: https://bit.ly/2Vi22xZ

14. Working poor experience financial crises due to COVID-19: https://n.pr/3cUCMX3

15. Working poor experience eight times higher job losses due to COVID-19: https://wapo.st/3cWXaGZ

16. German Chancellor Angela Merkel on the impact of the coronavirus: https://bit.ly/3dWm1uK

17. Fareed Zakaria on TED Connects: https://bit.ly/3e219SS

18. *New York Times*, Are We All In This Together? https://nyti.ms/2JYnGSZ

19. Canadian Prime Minister Justin Trudeau, our systems have been failing us for a long time: https://bit.ly/3cWdW9o

20. See footnote 1: Only 9.8% can achieve their dreams where they work

21. Residents not getting proper training: http://bit.ly/2pLczms

22. AR is Helping End Poverty by Delivering High-Quality Education in Myanmar http://bit.ly/32Wyj0U

23. Teachers working up to six jobs: https://cnn.it/2GoDaQA

24. Parsha, living out of her car: http://bit.ly/2uEkkPX

25. Taxi-Driver Suicides Are a Warning: http://bit.ly/2uBa1tL

26. World Economic Forum, Reskilling revolution required: http://bit.ly/2LekVvd

27. *Fortune* magazine President's Newsletter, June 1, 2018: Slow AI/Reskilling investments

28. Automation and the Changing Demand for Workforce Skills, Irving Wladawsky-Berger: https://on.wsj.com/2EkOnB8

29. *Fortune* CEO Newsletter, June 22, 2018: Fortune Business Roundtable

30. Work-from-home shift shocked companies: https://on.wsj.com/3iru0Ry

31. Dalio, Top 40%, Bottom 60% http://bit.ly/2GBgY5c. Also see https://theatln.tc/2pMlyUy , http://bit.ly/2pNQWkM , http://bit.ly/2GdM7fP , http://bit.ly/2IeOlHY , http://bit.ly/2E5x41I , https://fam.ag/2GGmfZh

32. Richest 1%: http://bit.ly/2GNPhHi

33. USA: Full-time minimum wage earners cannot afford to rent a two-bedroom apartment anywhere in the country http://bit.ly/2I1u6NL

34. Tech is Splitting the U.S. Workforce in Two: https://nyti.ms/2G9Ka3n

35. 40% of Americans are struggling to afford basics like food and shelter http://bit.ly/2RWubZF

36. *Fortune* CEO Newsletter, May 28, 2019: The Future of Capitalism

37. Humans Need Not Apply, video: http://bit.ly/2MoQwzd

38. Global useless class: https://nyti.ms/2pHgiRg

39. The Fourth Industrial Revolution is the biggest leap yet in mankind's relationship with his tools. In this revolution, digital, biological, and physical systems are coming together. Our tools and us are coming together as one: http://bit.ly/2JgobGu

40. Rage at globalism is just the beginning: https://for.tn/2HwGFFd

41. The Age of Primal Rage: http://bit.ly/2ILFnn5

42. Fear of Losing Status: http://bit.ly/2X2Wbf1

43. Futurist Stowe Boyd says current approaches are driving us towards an inevitable uprising: Human Spring, as he calls it. "The Human Spring will be caused by growing discontent in the Western industrialized nations, and the proximate causes are the rise of artificial intelligence and its impact on work, economic inequality, and panic about ecological catastrophe from climate change and the results of climate change, like the worldwide immigration crisis." http://bit.ly/2Je4SOS

44. (Why) Our Societies Need Healing: http://bit.ly/2AKYj2J

45. Why the 21st Century Needs (an Existential) Revolution: http://bit.ly/2YQB8NO

46. Reimaging Education in the Exponential Age: http://bit.ly/2I74ZuB

47. The Future of Jobs, 2018: World Economic Forum: http://bit.ly/2PS7sf0

48. Can The Selfie Generation Save Us? The Answer is Yes. http://bit.ly/2Kj3bSF

49. Activism isn't just for adults and teens, Caroline Paul: http://bit.ly/2NuR2IW

50. Video highlights of 11-14 year-old students' reactions to, and takeaways from, this book. Blue Sky School, Ottawa, Canada http://bit.ly/2KeZYn7

51. World Econmic Forum, "Our house is on fire": http://bit.ly/2yb2DGR

52. HP's CEO Dion Weisler is so passionate about diversity and inclusion, that he not only made it a corporate priority, he also mandated that all supplies in HP's supply chain had to meet the same D&I standards as HP, or they wouldn't do business with them. https://for.tn/2tbTY3U

53. The End of Shareholder Primacy: http://bit.ly/31TfZo1

54. The Business Roundtable Statement on the Purpose of a Corporation: http://bit.ly/2z7ujwH

55. Dr. King fierce urgency of now speech: http://bit.ly/2r3161B

56. Congressman John Lewis, Good trouble: https://bit.ly/2SqjyPP

57. Great Law of the Iroquois Confederacy: http://bit.ly/2KYGx2j

58. St. Benedict's Prep teaches self-management: http://bit.ly/2pcqe6R

59. Modeling the Impact of AI on the World Economy https://mck.co/2Q3xuwR

60. McKinsey: Jobs Lost, Jobs Gained: What the future of work will mean for jobs, skills, wages: https://mck.co/2yIWph4

61. Amazon pledges to upskill 100,000 employees: http://bit.ly/2LHLOfl

62. *Fortune* CEO Newsletter, November 5, 2018: The Social Implications of AI

63. Priya Parker TED talk on transformative conversations: http://bit.ly/2KCjUke

64. MIT Disobedience Award: http://bit.ly/2xaoKww

65. IDEO, Bridging the Gap Between the Future and Business Reality: http://bit.ly/2XJPse9

About Bill, Yuko, Mihato

BILL JENSEN

Bill Jensen makes it easier to do great work. He helps companies and teams double their productivity and pursue their passions.

Bill Jensen makes it easier to leap into tomorrow. He is an IBM Futurist and has conducted high-impact future of work research for multiple technology giants.

He has spent the past 30 years studying how work gets done. Over 1,000,000 people across the globe interviewed and surveyed. (Much of what he's found horrifies him.)

Bill is an internationally-acclaimed thought leader who is known for extremely useful content, with a passion for making it easier for everyone to work smarter, not harder.

His books:

- *Simplicity*
- *Work 2.0*
- *Simplicity Survival Handbook*
- *What Is Your Life's Work?*
- *Hacking Work*
- *The Courage Within Us*
- *Disrupt!*
- *Future Strong*
- *The Day Tomorrow Said No*

Bill is CEO of The Jensen Group, a change consulting firm he founded in 1985; serving half of the Fortune 250, plus startups, midsize firms, armed forces, governments, and nonprofits. He lives in Morristown, New Jersey, travels the world for clients and sneaks in fun time wherever he goes.

bill@simplerwork.com   www.simplerwork.com   @simpletonbill

YUKO FUKUSHIMA

Yuko Fukushima is an art director, concept artist and designer from Japan, currently based in Berlin. She travels to work from anywhere, creates mixed-media works in a shared studio in Kreuzberg, and eats way too much cilantro.

mail@yukoarts.com   https://hi.yuko.im   @hiyukoim

MIHATO

Mihato is currently living in Japan. She's an illustrator with experiences in game layout and concept art design. Started her career around 2015 and has been involved mainly but not limited to the gaming field, and is continuing to expand her activity.

383838ta@gmail.com Twitter: @383838ta114
Instagram: @mihato

THE DISCOVERY
THAT FOREVER CHANGED THE FUTURE
AND HOW WE WORK

Bill Jensen

Visit www.tomorrowsaidy.es and www.simplerwork.com for more